FOCUS ON
Writing Composition 2

Ray Barker   Louis Fidge

	FICTION											NON-FICTION					
	Historical texts	Plays	Imagined worlds	Sci-fi/fantasy	Dilemmas and issues	Stories from other cultures	Classic poetry	Modern poetry	Poems from different cultures	Poems from different times	Range of poetic forms	Reports	Instructions	Information texts	Explanations	Persuasive writing	Discussion texts
			✓		✓												
	✓		✓														
		✓															
							✓			✓							
	✓		✓	✓													
												✓					✓
													✓				
												✓		✓			
				✓													
							✓		✓	✓	✓						
			✓	✓													
															✓		✓
														✓	✓		
				✓	✓												
				✓	✓												
							✓			✓							
						✓	✓			✓							
																✓	✓
																✓	✓
														✓			✓
																✓	

Contents

Unit 1	Character Sketches	page 4
Unit 2	What Would *You* Do?	6
Unit 3	Writing a Playscript	8
Unit 4	Writing Poetry	10
Unit 5	Writing in Paragraphs	12
Unit 6	Writing a Newspaper Report	14
Unit 7	Writing Instructions	16
Unit 8	Writing a Report	18
Unit 9	Writing about Settings	20
Unit 10	Poetry from the Past	22
Unit 11	Using Descriptive Language	24
Unit 12	Making Notes	26
Unit 13	Charts and Diagrams	28
Unit 14	Writing Explanations	30
Unit 15	Moral Dilemmas	32
Unit 16	Story Endings	34
Unit 17	Alphabet Poems and Acrostics	36
Unit 18	Conversation Poems	38
Unit 19	Expressing a Point of View	40
Unit 20	Writing a Letter	42
Unit 21	Writing a Summary	44
Unit 22	Composing an Advertisement	46

UNIT 1   Character Sketches

> **Think ahead**
>
> We can learn a lot about characters by their appearance, and the things they say and the way they act.

Amy felt so excited. She threw open the door, bursting to tell her Mum the news about the school trip. "Mum. You'll never guess what …" she began, but her voice trailed off and the smile faded from her face as she saw her Gran sitting at the table with her Mum, drinking tea. Gran, dressed completely in black, looked small and shrivelled but her eyes glinted as she stared steadily at Amy. In the corner of the room, Amy noticed a battered old suitcase.

"Don't they teach you manners at school these days?" her Gran snapped. "It's rude to burst in and interrupt a conversation." Amy saw her Mum draw in her breath as if she were about to say something, and then saw her shoulders droop and a resigned look appear on her face. Her Mum never interfered when Gran said anything.

"Sorry, Gran," Amy muttered.

"And just look at the state of your school uniform. You look so scruffy." Gran never seemed to say a good word about anyone or anything. Amy had never seen her smile.

Amy tried to change the subject. "How is your bad back, today, Gran?" she asked.

Gran loved to moan and groan about her aches and pains. Sometimes she would go on for ages.

Before she could reply, Amy's Mum spoke up. "Gran's not been feeling too well lately, so she has come to stay with us for a few weeks," Amy's Mum said. "She'll be staying in the spare bedroom."

4

Thinking back

1 Name the three characters in the passage.
2 Write some things you know about Gran's appearance.
3 Do you like Gran's character? Give your reasons.
4 What can you tell about Gran by the things she says?
5 Which of these words do you think best describe Gran:
      thoughtful, kind, selfish, hurtful, nasty, complaining.
6 What do you think Amy and her Mum think of Gran? Say why.

Thinking about it

1 Write some of the things you think Gran might say about:
   a) pop music   b) Amy's choice of clothes   c) television
2 Write and say how you think Gran might behave:
   a) on a crowded bus   b) at the doctors   c) in the supermarket
3 Write a character sketch of one of your grandparents (or a relative you know well).

Thinking it through

1 In fairy stories, we often think of characters in a particular way. Princesses are beautiful, gentle, innocent but queens are jealous, wicked, vain. Write some words to describe each of the following characters:
   a) giants   b) wizards   c) kings   d) dragons
2 Choose one of the characters you have described. Write some paragraphs showing the character behaving:
   a) in a manner you would expect   b) very differently from expected.
   (Use copymaster 1.)

Stepping Stones to help you

- When describing characters write about :
   – their appearance   – things they do and say   – other interesting facts
- Use good describing words
(Use copymaster F.)

5

UNIT 2   What Would *You* Do?

> ### Think ahead
>
> *Have you ever been really scared? Read the passage and imagine you are Ninny, hiding.*

I crept up carefully into a bed of rusty bracken and peeped out. On both sides of the valley were masses of soldiers on horses. Different coloured flags were flapping wetly on each side, but all the soldiers looked the same to me. The same round shields, the same long spears, the same sort of armour.

From each side, a party of horsemen was riding towards the middle ground. Towards me. Were they going to fight? No, from each party a man got off his horse and walked forwards, carrying a green branch. Some of the others dismounted too.

These men didn't trust each other. They were like dogs, walking stiff-legged around each other before a dog-fight begins. The two men in the middle were going to talk. But I didn't see much hope of peace, with all those soldiers about.

One man handed the reins of his horse to another and started walking straight towards my bracken clump.

I froze. Easy enough – I'd been freezing for a long time.

I was going to sneeze!

I bottled it up, but it escaped in a kind of hiss.

Without thinking, the soldier pulled out his sword and took a swipe at the bushes. I toppled back into the ditch and he missed me. I don't know if he saw me or not, but it didn't matter. That swipe at the bushes started the battle.

I huddled at the bottom of the wet ditch and heard shouts of rage, sounds of swords.

From *Ninny's Boat* by Clive King

Thinking back

1 Where was Ninny hiding?
2 Who were on both sides of the valley?
3 What made Ninny think there was going to be a battle?
4 a) How do you think Ninny felt when the soldier walked straight towards him?
　b) What thoughts do you think went through Ninny's head at this moment?
5 Explain what started the battle.

Thinking about it

1 What do you think happens next in the story? In rough, write down a few possibilities. Choose one of them and continue the story.
2 (Use copymaster 2.)

Thinking it through

1 Think of a time when you were really scared. Explain what happened.
2 Imagine that you are just coming home from the shops and you see someone trying to break into your house. Describe what you see. What thoughts race through your mind? What do you feel? What would you do? Would you:
　– hide and watch? What happens?
　– try to stop the burglar? What happens?
　– tell someone? What would you say? What happens?

UNIT 3 Writing a Playscript

> **Think ahead**
> How do actors know what to say and do in a play?

Setting The play takes place a long time ago, late at night at an inn in Bethlehem.

Narrator It has been a busy day. Just as the innkeeper is finishing his supper, there is a knock at the door. When he opens it, the innkeeper sees a pregnant woman on a donkey being led by a bearded man.

Innkeeper No room.

Joseph But we're tired and have travelled through night and day.

Innkeeper There's only the stable round the back.

(*The innkeeper indicates with his hand. Joseph nods.*)

Here's two blankets. Sign the register.

(*Mary and Joseph take the blankets, sign the register and exit.*)

Narrator The innkeeper shuts the door, climbs the stairs and gets tiredly into bed. Soon he is fast asleep. But then there is another knock at the door. Frowning, the innkeeper gets up, and opens the door.

Joseph Excuse me. I wonder if you could lend us another, smaller blanket?

(*The innkeeper gives Joseph another blanket. Joseph exits.*)

Narrator The innkeeper shuts the door, climbs the stairs and once more gets into bed and goes to sleep. Then a bright light wakes him up.

Innkeeper (*sounding fed up*) That's all I need!

Narrator The innkeeper gets up, draws the curtains to block out the light and then goes back to sleep.

Thinking back

1. Where does the play take place? How do you know?
2. Name the characters mentioned.
3. How does each character know when to speak?
4. How do the words, written in *italics* in the brackets, help the actors?
5. What is the job of the narrator?

Thinking about it

Copy and complete how you think the next part of the play goes.

Narrator But then there is **another** knock at the door. Mumbling angrily, the innkeeper opens the door and finds three shepherds standing there.

Innkeeper
Shepherds
Innkeeper
Narrator

Thinking it through

1. Read the complete story on which the play is based. (Use copymaster 3.) Explain how the first part of the story has been adapted and changed slightly to make it into a playscript.
2. Write the rest of the story as a playscript. Adapt it as necessary. Use the Stepping Stones below to help you.

Stepping Stones to help you

- Write the characters' names clearly.
- Start a new line each time a new character speaks.
- Use a narrator to tell parts of the story.
- Include instructions to actors in brackets.

(Use copymaster D.)

UNIT 4   Writing Poetry

> **Think ahead**
>
> Do you ever lie in bed and listen to the wind blowing? In the poem, notice the way the poet uses interesting verbs to describe the sounds it makes.

When the wind blows
The quiet things speak.
Some whisper, some clang,
Some creak.

Grasses swish.
Treetops sigh.
Flags slap
and snap at the sky.
Wires on poles
whistle and hum.
Ashcans roll.
Windows drum.

When the wind goes—
suddenly
then,
the quiet things
are quiet again.

From 'Wind Song' by Lilian Moore

Thinking back

1. How many verses are there?
2. How many lines are there in each verse?
3. Write a sentence and explain how the poem rhymes.
4. Copy the poem. Underline the verbs in it.

Thinking about it

1. Think of some verbs to describe the sound each thing makes in the wind.
   a) tin cans <u>clatter</u> b) leaves c) doors
   d) paper e) cardboard boxes f) washing on the line
   g) window panes h) dustbin lids i) stairs
2. Experiment with the poem. Rewrite the poem and replace some of the verbs.
   For example: When the wind <u>howls</u> the quiet things <u>moan</u>.
                 Some <u>grunt</u>, some <u>growl</u>, some <u>groan</u>.
   Use the Stepping Stones below to help you.

Thinking it through

1. Write down some scary sounds that you might hear when you are lying in bed at night. For example: the creaking floorboards, the hoot of an owl, the murmur of voices, screeching cats on the prowl. Make them into a list poem of rhyming pairs, like this:
   The hoot of an owl,
   Cats on the prowl.
2. Use some of your ideas to make up a poem of your own, called "One cold windy night".
   (Use copymaster 4.)

Stepping Stones to help you

- Firstly, brainstorm ideas and jot them down in rough.
- Experiment with them. Don't be afraid to change them.
- Choose your best ideas and make a best copy of your piece of work.

(Use copymaster C.)

11

UNIT 5 Writing in Paragraphs

> ### Think ahead
> A paragraph is a group of sentences about the same idea. Paragraphs help to break up a piece of writing into smaller chunks and make it easier to read. Sam was given these pictures. She made the notes below as part of her story plan. She is going to write a paragraph about each. How many paragraphs will she write?

Jim Hawkins – explorer – storm – shipwreck – abandon ship

swim – reach desert island – exhausted

collect leaves, branches – make fire – make shelter

explore – look for food and water – success!

Thinking back

1 What is Sam's story going to be about?
2 Who is the main character?
3 Where does the story take place?
4 Will the story be set in the past or the present? How do you know?
5 What sort of a person do you think Jim is?
6 a) How do you think Jim would be feeling?
  b) What thoughts would be going through his head?

 Thinking about it

1 Here is Sam's first paragraph.
   Jim Hawkins was terrified. The raging storm had capsized his sailing boat. It was sinking fast. All thoughts of exploring left his mind – his life itself was in danger. Jim looked towards the island in the distance. It was his only hope. He took a deep breath and plunged into the icy sea.
   Write a short paragraph for each of the other parts of Sam's plan.
2 Continue the story in your own words. Write four more paragraphs. (Use copymaster 5.)

 Thinking it through

- If possible, work with a friend.
- Draw a map of a desert island.
- Include some of the following places on it: a swamp, a jungle, a deserted village, a volcano, a river with dangerous rapids and a waterfall, sinking sands, a lagoon, a coral reef, a bay, some cliffs with caves.
- Make up your own names for each place (such as Fire Mountain, Wrecker's Reef). Imagine Jim Hawkins exploring some of the places on the island. Plan and write a chapter about his adventures at each place.
- Use Sam's idea of pictures or notes to help you write each chapter in paragraphs.

UNIT 6 Writing a Newspaper Report

> **Think ahead**
> How can you tell this is going to be a newspaper report?

BEASTLY BLESSINGS

St Marks Church was a little like Noah's ark yesterday – full of rats, cats and other animals. The event was a blessing of the animals by the Reverend Ralph Rutherford at his church in London. Animal blessing services are steadily growing in popularity. Mr Rutherford said "All animals are part of God's creation. They provide companionship and comfort to many."

"I would not miss this service for the world," said one local resident, holding a rather handsome black cat. "It makes an outing for Silky. Round here the animals can only go out if you are with them. It's terribly dangerous for them on their own with all the traffic."

Four rats, belonging to Joseph Davidson, proved to be the star attraction. "I think rats are so lovely," said a pretty blond girl. Joseph put one of the rodents on her shoulder, where it promptly tangled itself in her hair.

During the service, the Reverend Rutherford blessed the animals by flicking holy water over them. "The rats are scared of water," cried Joseph, moving to protect them with his anorak. But the creatures got sprayed anyway and did not seem to mind at all.

The singing of the well-known hymn, *All Things Bright and Beautiful* brought the service to a close. The street outside soon filled with people, chatting and smiling to each other as they took their newly-blessed animals home.

Thinking back

1. What is the report all about?
2. a) What is the headline?   b) Do you think it is clever? Why?
3. Is the report set out in lines across the page or in columns?
4. How many paragraphs are there in the report?
5. The opening paragraph sets the scene. What does it tell you?
6. Name the different people interviewed in the report.
7. Write ten facts you have discovered from the report.

 Thinking about it

Choose one of the following and write a newspaper report about:
– something unusual or exciting you have seen or done at school or at home, such as the school sports day, Christmas play or an experiment that went wrong!
– somewhere you have visited. It can be true or imaginary.
Use the Stepping Stones below and the report opposite to help you. (See copymaster 6 to help plan the report.)

 Thinking it through

1. Write a newspaper report about the animal blessing service – but change it to include something that went very wrong!
2. Write a newspaper report based on an incident from a story you have read or know well, such as The Gingerbread Man.

Stepping Stones to help you

- Think of an interesting headline.
- Set the article out in paragraphs.
- Include
  – a photograph or picture
  – some interesting facts and descriptions.
  – some quotations from people involved.

UNIT 7   Writing Instructions

> **Think ahead**
>
> *As you read the instructions, think about what it is that makes them easy to follow.*

How to recycle paper

What you need
- some sheets of newspaper
- a bucket and some water
- some old material
- something heavy

What you do

Step 1   Tear the newspaper into small pieces, and put it into the water in the bucket.

Step 2   Soak it in water for a few hours.

Step 3   Squeeze out the excess water from the paper.

Step 4   Squash the pulped paper onto a piece of old material on a flat surface.

Step 5   Lay another piece of material on top of the pulped paper.

Step 6   Place something heavy on top of everything to flatten the paper.

Step 7   When the paper is flattened, take the weight and the material off the top, and leave the paper to dry.

Step 8   When it is dry, why not use the paper to make a card for someone special?

Thinking back

1. What are the instructions for?
2. The instructions opposite are divided into two sections.
   a) What is the first section called?
   b) Why is this important?
   c) What is the purpose of the second section?
   d) How does the layout of this section help you?
   e) Can you think of a way of improving this section?

Thinking about it

Choose one of the topics below and write a set of clear instructions. Use the instructions on the opposite page, and any other ideas of your own, to help you set out your instructions clearly.
a) making a cup of tea   b) bathing a dog   c) planning a story

Thinking it through

1. Explain clearly how to play noughts and crosses. Use the following headings to help you:
   - Aim of the game
   - Number of players
   - What you need
   - What you do.
   (Use copymaster 7.)
2. Use the copymaster to help you explain how to play a simple board game, such as Snakes and Ladders or Draughts.

Stepping Stones to help you

- Write the aim first.
- Next write what is needed.
- Then write clear steps on what you have to do.

(Use copymaster H.)

17

UNIT 8   Writing a Report

> **Think ahead**
>
> How do the headings in the report below help you?

Naqish was asked to write a report on where he lived.

REPORT ON LUTON

Location
Luton is in the county of Bedfordshire, in England. It is about 30 miles north of London.

Size
Luton has a population of around 100,000 people of different nationalities.

Transport Links
One of the country's main motorways, the M1, runs near Luton. The town is 40 minutes from London by train. At Luton bus station you can catch local buses or coaches to take you all over the country. From Luton Airport you can fly to other UK cities and overseas.

Employment
Luton has many industries. Much employment in the town is connected with the airport and a large car factory. There are many other kinds of jobs linked to Luton's many offices and shops.

Sport and Leisure
Good sports and leisure facilities may be found in the Town. Luton has its own football club. There are several cinemas, libraries and leisure centres as well as a local theatre.

Final Comment
Luton is a good place to live. There is so much to see and do.

Thinking back

1. What is the report about?
2. Write five different facts you have discovered from the report.
3. Name the different sections the report is divided into.
4. What does the final section tell you about Naqish's view of Luton?
5. Think of some other sections Naqish might have included, such as something on the history of the town.

 Thinking about it

Write a report on the city, town or village where you live.
Use copymaster 8 to help you plan it in rough first, and then make a best copy.

 Thinking it through

Choose one of the following topics and write a report on it.
a) my school
b) a hobby or interest
c) a favourite sport or sport's team
d) a pop group
e) a favourite animal
Use the Stepping Stones below to help you plan it.

Stepping Stones to help you

- Write notes on all you know, or can find out, about the subject.
- Organise your notes under suitable headings.
- Write your report in rough first.
- Write a few sentences for each heading.
- Re-read your draft for mistakes and write a best copy.

(Use copymaster E.)

UNIT 9 Writing about Settings

> **Think ahead**
>
> *Choosing your words carefully can help you create an atmosphere and build up a picture of the setting in the reader's mind. How successful do you think this description is?*

Voyager 7 touched down on Planet Delta. Captain Nimmo switched on the scanner and studied the landscape.

Three suns glowed in the golden sky like flickering lanterns on a summer evening. A range of rounded, rolling hills were outlined softly against the warm glow. All around the spacecraft the ground was covered with a thick carpet of soft green moss, sprinkled with beautiful orange flowers, scattered like confetti. The deep red leaves of tall slender plants whispered and rustled in a light breeze. Captain Nimmo pointed out a group of small furry creatures, who were waving and smiling welcomingly at the crew of the spacecraft.

"It looks a friendly place," Captain Nimmo said. "Let's go and explore."

Thinking back

1. a) Where is the story set?
   b) Who is the main character?
   c) Why do you think the spacecraft has landed on Planet Delta?
2. Does the planet look a friendly or an unfriendly place?
3. Copy the description of the planet (from "Three suns glowed in the golden sky …") Underline the words and phrases that give the setting a friendly feel.

Thinking about it

Imagine Planet Delta is an unfriendly, hostile place. Use the Stepping Stones to help you write a description of what Captain Nimmo might have seen.
Here are some things you could include:
   suns, sky, clouds, lightning, mountains, craters, caves, rocks, plants, aliens.
Do it something like this:
   A ridge of twisted, angry-looking mountains, belching choking black smoke, stood out starkly against the grey skyline.

Thinking it through

1. Imagine you are on a boat at sea. Write a description of a calm day and a description of a storm.
2. Write a description of a wood on a summer's day. Now write a description of the same wood on a cloudless, cold, dark night.
3. Use copymaster 9 to help you compare contrasting settings.

Stepping Stones to help you

- Try to picture the setting in your mind.
- List some things you see, hear, smell and feel.
- Use interesting words to make the description come 'alive'.
- Don't be afraid to experiment with the words and language you use.

(Use copymaster B.)

UNIT 10 Poetry from the Past

> ### Think ahead
>
> Poems written in the past often contain some unusual words, or may be written in an unusual way. Read the poem several times to help you work out the meaning. Try tapping out the rhythm of the poem as you read it.

Swift of foot was Hiawatha;
He could shoot an arrow from him,
And run forward with such fleetness,
That the arrow fell behind him!

Strong of arm was Hiawatha;
He could shoot ten arrows upward,
Shoot them with such strength and swiftness,
That the tenth had left the bowstring
Ere the first to earth had fallen!

He had mittens, Minjekahwun,
Magic mittens made of deerskin;
When upon his hands he wore them,
He could smite the rocks asunder,
He could grind them into powder.

He had moccasins enchanted,
Magic moccasins made of deerskin;
When he bound them round his ankles,
When upon his feet he tied them,
At each stride a mile he measured!

From *The Song of Hiawatha* by Henry Wadsworth Longfellow

Thinking back

1. The first verse tells us that Hiawatha could run very _____ .
2. Which two words mean 'fast' in verse 1?
3. The second verse tells us that Hiawatha was very _____ .
4. What proved he was very strong and fast in verse 2?
5. The third verse tells us about Hiawatha's magic _____ .
6. What does 'smite the rocks asunder' mean?
7. The fourth verse tells us about Haiwatha's magic _____ .
8. How long was each stride when he wore the moccasins?

Thinking about it

1. Imagine Hiawatha also had other special powers. List some of the things you think he would be able to do if he was:
   a) sharp of sight   b) keen of hearing   c) loud of voice
2. Imagine Hiawatha wore some more magical things. List some of the things he would be able to do when he wore his:
   a) magical mask   b) magical belt   c) magical feathers

Thinking it through

Read the poem opposite again. Then use some of your ideas from the 'Thinking about it' section. Turn them into extra verses for the poem. Don't worry about rhyming, but try to keep to the same rhythm as the original poem in the verses you write. (Use copymaster 10 to help plan the verses.)

Stepping Stones to help you

- Firstly, brainstorm ideas and jot them down in rough.
- Experiment with them. Don't be afraid to cross them out or change them.
- Choose your best ideas and make a best copy of your piece of work.

(Use copymaster C.)

UNIT 11   Using Descriptive Language

> ### Think ahead
> The author has used some interesting descriptive words and phrases in the passage below. Compare the scene at the beginning and the end of the passage. How are they different?

People said that once, long ago, there had been a village on the sands, but that one day there had been a flood and the sea had covered it up. People said that the village was still there and that some days the church bells could still be heard beneath the sea.

The sky was as black as night all day long, and the wind blew so hard that it drove a strong man backwards, and the thunder growled and crackled so that we had to make signs to each other, for talking was no use, and the lightning flashed so bright that my mother could thread her needle by it. My mother was frightened, but my father said, "I think it will come out all right." And so it did. The sky cleared up for a beautiful evening, and the sun turned all the vast wet sands to a sheet of gold as far as the eye could see. The sea had been driven back so far that it had vanished out of sight. And there, far, far across the golden beach, lay a tiny village, shining in the setting sun.

　I began to run towards it, and all the other children followed me. As we drew nearer, the little houses became plainer, looking like blocks of gold in the evening light.

Taken from 'The Sea-Baby' by Eleanor Farjeon
(from *The Old Nurse's Stocking Basket*)

Thinking back

1. **Copy and finish these sentences.**
   a) The wind blew so hard that _____ .
   b) The lightning flashed so bright that _____ .
2. **Copy and fill in the missing descriptive words.**
   a) The sky was as _____ as _____ .
   b) The thunder _____ and _____ .
   c) The little houses looked like _____ of _____ .
3. Find and write some more descriptive phrases from the passage.

Thinking about it

1. **Copy and fill in the gaps with suitable descriptive words.**
   As we approached the lost village the _____ streets looked like _____ . The _____ church steeple pointed to the sky like a _____ . There were soft colours everywhere – pink, yellow, _____ and _____ . _____ flowers sprang up and covered the ground like a _____ . Bees _____ busily.
2. Continue the description. Think of other things you might see (like the village school and shop). What other sounds might you hear, for example the church bells, laughter? Choose your words carefully. Use 'describing' words such as similes.

Thinking it through

1. Imagine you explored a building and found a tunnel to an underground cave. Describe what you saw.
2. (Use copymaster 11.)

Stepping Stones to help you

- Is there anything you want to cross out or change?
- Have you punctuated your work correctly?
- Have you checked for silly spelling mistakes?

(Use copymaster M.)

UNIT 12 Making Notes

> **Think ahead**
>
> Attif has made some notes by underlining the most important words in the first paragraph. Do you agree with his choice of words?

Helen loses her sight and hearing

<u>Helen Keller</u> was <u>born</u> in <u>America</u> in <u>1880</u>, but two years later, in <u>1882</u>, she was struck by a mystery illness. Suddenly, after a perfectly normal start to life, she <u>lost</u> her <u>sight and hearing</u>. As she got older, her inability to communicate made her angry and she <u>became a very naughty child</u>. Her <u>parents</u> did not know how to help her so they <u>employed</u> a <u>teacher to help Helen</u>.

Ann Sullivan comes to help

Ann Sullivan was a patient person. She soon won Helen's confidence by her firm, but caring approach. Helen began to calm down, and soon became an obedient and loving child.

Ann gradually began to help Helen communicate. She taught Helen the hand alphabet. Helen learned that everything had a name and that she could express herself by spelling out words with her hands. Later on, Helen learned to read and write by using Braille (raised letters in the form of dots which Helen 'read' by running her fingers over the dots). At last, Helen began to be able to lead a more normal life. She even learned to speak and was able to attend college.

<u>Attif's notes</u>
Helen Keller – born 1880 – America – 1882 lost sight and hearing – became very naughty child – parents employed teacher to help Helen.

26

Thinking back

1. a) What is the heading of the first paragraph and second paragraph?
   b) Make up a sensible heading for the third paragraph.
2. Copy the second paragraph. Underline the most important words in it.
3. Write some notes for the second paragraph (like Attif's).
4. Make notes on the third paragraph.
5. Write some proper sentences based on these notes:
   Helen helped poor and disabled – raised money through books, films and concerts – died 1968.

Thinking about it

1. Make these notes about Florence Nightingale into proper sentences.
   Florence Nightingale – born 1820 – wealthy family – wanted to be nurse – parents objected – Florence ran away to train as nurse – 1854 sent to help soldiers hurt in battle – worked tirelessly – difficult circumstances – soldiers loved her – became famous.
2. Use copymaster 12 to practise your note-making skills.

Thinking it through

1. Use the notes from this description to:
   a) draw a picture of the person they describe
   b) write a description using proper sentences.
      pointed chin – glasses – blue eyes – bald head – scar on left cheek – ear-ring in right ear – missing front tooth – rarely smiles.
2. Choose someone from your class. Make notes on their appearance. Do not give their name. Can others recognise the person from just your notes?

UNIT 13 Charts and Diagrams

> **Think ahead**
>
> We can often represent information in the form of charts or diagrams with labels. How do you think this helps?

The Sun

The Sun is at the centre of our solar system. The Sun controls the movements of all the planets. Although it is 150 million kilometres from Earth, it is our nearest star. The Sun takes nearly four weeks to revolve. The Sun does not have a solid crust, like the Earth, but is made of extremely hot gases, mainly hydrogen. Without its heat, nothing could survive on Earth.

The Earth

Our Earth depends on the Sun for heat. By comparison with the Sun, our Earth is very small – it is one million times smaller than the Sun! The Earth revolves once every 24 hours. The side which faces the Sun is in light, and the side which faces away from it, is in darkness. This is why we have day and night. It takes one year for the Earth to revolve around the Sun.

The Moon

The Moon is smaller than the Earth. It revolves around the Earth, and takes about four weeks to do so. The Moon has no atmosphere. It has no water either, but there are large flat areas, which we call 'seas'! There are many craters on the surface of the Moon.

Thinking back

Draw a chart like the one below and use the information on the opposite page to fill in four facts you have discovered about each:

The Sun	The Earth	The Moon

Thinking about it

1 Copy these diagrams. Fill in the missing information.

a) b) c)

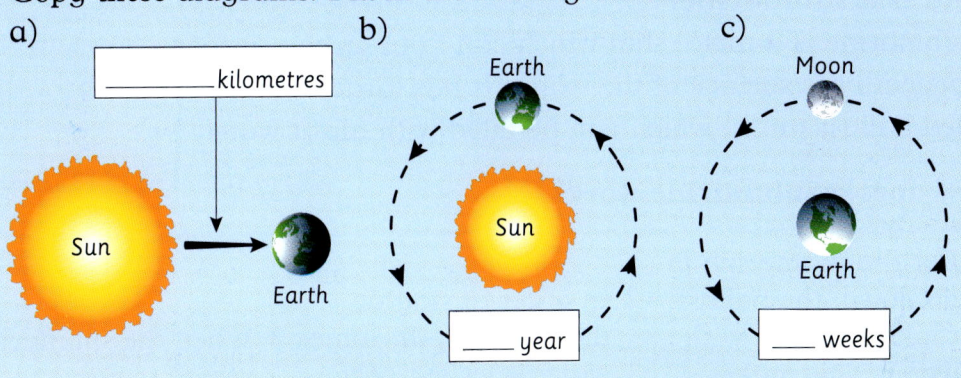

2 Use copymaster 13 for further labelling activities.

Thinking it through

Use the information below to help you complete the flow diagram. (Work out how many boxes you need to draw first!)

Scientists believe that the Sun started off as a cloud of gas. The middle of the cloud became very hot. The Sun was formed. In millions of years the centre of the Sun will be used up and it will no longer give out heat. The Sun will get smaller. All life on Earth will cease. The Sun will eventually collapse.

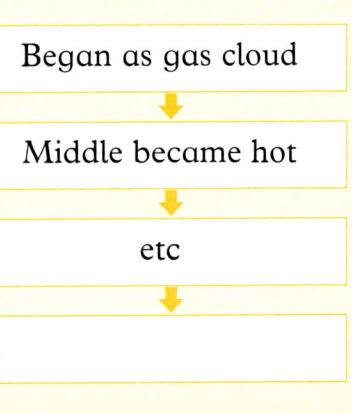

29

UNIT 14 Writing Explanations

> **Think ahead**
>
> When you explain something, you should do so as clearly as possible. How easy to follow is this explanation? Why?

SUBMARINES

Introduction
Submarines are used for exploring under the sea.

What is a submarine?
A submarine is a metal ship which can float on the surface or beneath the surface of the water. It has large tanks, called ballast tanks, which can be filled with air or water.

How does a submarine work?

1 For the submarine to go down, the ballast tanks are filled with water. This makes the submarine heavy so it sinks.

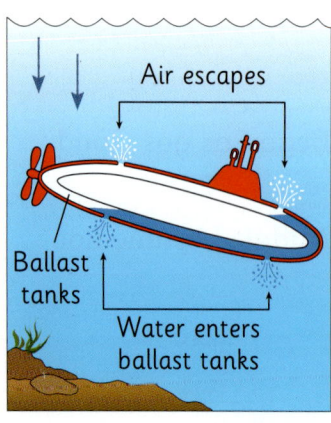

2 In order to stay at the same depth, some water is let out of the ballast tanks into the sea. The tanks are then partly filled with water and partly filled with air. This makes them lighter.

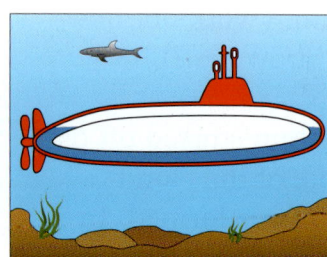

3 When the submarine wishes to come to the surface, it empties all the water from the ballast tanks, and fills it with air. This makes the submarine light, so it rises to the surface.

Interesting comment
The prefix 'sub' means 'under' and the word 'marine' means 'the sea'. 'Submarine' therefore means 'under the sea'.

Thinking back

1 a) What is the explanation all about?
  b) How can you tell, even before you read it?
2 a) Name the sections that the explanation is divided into.
  b) How does this help make it easier to read?
3 In the section on 'How does a submarine work?' how do the diagrams and numbers help you?

 Thinking about it

1 Choose one of the following and explain how it works
  a) a pair of scissors or b) a pencil sharpener.
  Use the explanation opposite and the Stepping Stones below, to help you set out your explanation.
2 Explain how a lock on a canal works. (Use copymaster 14.)

 Thinking it through

1 Imagine you met an alien from outer space. Explain traffic lights to the alien.
2 Name a favourite sports team or pop group. Explain something about who they are and what they do. Give several reasons why you like them. Think of an interesting comment to finish with.

Stepping Stones to help you

- Write what you are going to try to explain.
- Organise your explanation into clear steps or paragraphs.
- Use numbering or labelled diagrams, if necessary.

(Use copymaster N.)

UNIT 15 Moral Dilemmas

> **Think ahead**
>
> We all have to face problems and make difficult decisions sometimes. Read the introduction. What moral dilemma do you think Joshua will face?

Joshua was a Maori boy. (Maories were the first people to live in New Zealand.) He had just started school away from his own people. He makes some new 'friends' at school – but are they 'real' friends?

"You thirsty?" Shane looked at Joshua and winked at Glen.

"Yes," said Joshua. "Yeah. O.K."

"Let's try old Rama's dairy," said Glen.

"No money," said Joshua.

"Don't need any," said Glen.

The boys stood around outside the dairy. Joshua wondered why they waited so long. He wondered why they sort of hid to one side just outside the door.

"He's gone out the back. Now," said Shane. "Go on, Joshie, that fridge over there. Three Cokes. Get them quick and bring them out." He pointed to the drink cooler.

"Get a move on," said Glen. "He won't stay out the back all day."

"Money," said Joshua.

"Go on," said Shane. "Don't need no money."

Joshua looked at the other two and knew what they wanted him to do. He wanted to say no but he didn't know how. They were his friends. They had asked him to play.

"Now," said Glen. "We'll wait here." He pushed at Joshua.

Joshua waited for a moment and then went into the shop. He could not see Mr Rama. He looked back over his shoulder and could not see Glen or Shane either.

From *The Magpies Said* by William Taylor

Thinking back

1. Who are the three main characters in the passage?
2. Where does the passage take place?
3. What can you tell about Glen and Shane from the passage?
4. Does Joshua want to go into the shop? How can you tell?
5. Why does Joshua do as he is told?
6. a) How do you think Joshua is feeling?
   b) What do you think he is thinking?
7. What choices does he have at this point?

Thinking about it

1. List at least three different ways the story could develop. (Don't forget to include some unexpected events – life isn't always predictable!)
2. Choose one of them and continue the story.
3. When you have finished, read how the author continued the story (use copymaster 15). Write what you think of the author's ending. Explain what you liked, or disliked, about it.

Thinking it through

1. Think about a moral dilemma you have had to face. Explain what it was, where you were, who was involved and write what happened.
2. Choose one of these ideas. Write a short story.
   a) Tom and his sister Sam have gone to the park to play. They have taken their dog Tug with them. They get involved with their friends. Tug wanders off. They promised to be home by 7.30. It is now 8.00 and the dog is nowhere to be found. What should they do?
   b) Shireen is walking home. As she passes an alley she sees a gang of older children picking on her best friend friend Nasi. She knows these children are bullies, and enjoy picking on smaller children. Shireen knows they are stronger than she is. What should she do?

33

UNIT 16 Story Endings

Think ahead

The way a story ends can make a lot of difference. The ending may be happy, sad, unexpected, exciting, mysterious. Read the introduction to the story and guess how it might end.

Floella had come all the way to England from Trinidad on the boat with her brothers and sisters. She had not seen her parents for fifteen months. As the ship got closer Floella looked desperately for her 'Marmie' in the crowds at the dock.

Suddenly, there she was, beaming with joy like an angel, waving frantically. There was a man beside her who was not my father. I could see her talking to him and pointing us out. Eventually, when the ship was anchored, he came on board up the gangway. He made his way over to us and introduced himself. He was a social worker whose job it was to meet passengers as they arrived and to help those who needed advice about how to get to their new destination. He looked after us because Marmie was not allowed to come on board and as we were children travelling alone he took charge of us. He bundled all our luggage together and swiftly pushed past the other passengers, the four of us in tow behind him. My heart pounded loudly as thunder as I climbed down the gangplank, this time not with fear but with joy as I ran towards Marmie.

  We all made a dash for her and hugged her. She squeezed us so tightly I felt I would break. The love and joy that passed through every bit of our bodies was overwhelming. I was at last in paradise, clutching Marmie. I never wanted to be away from her again. I was back with my beloved Marmie at long last.

From *Coming to England* by Floella Benjamin

Thinking back

1. a) Who is telling the story?
   b) Where was she at the start of the passage?
   c) What was she doing?
   d) Why was she nervous?
2. What sort of ending did the story have?
3. Write and say what you liked, or disliked, about the ending.
4. How did Marmie feel when she saw Floella? How do you know?
5. How do you know Floella was pleased to see her mother? Copy some of the words or phrases the author uses to describe her feelings.

 Thinking about it

1. Describe the scene on the boat as it approached the dock. What would Floella have seen and heard? How would she have felt? What thoughts would have been going through her mind? What would she be doing?
2. Write a different ending to the story. Imagine that there had been nobody to meet Floella. How would she have felt then? What would she have thought? What could have happened? What would she have done?
3. Use copymaster 16 for more ideas about making up different endings for stories.

 Thinking it through

- Think of a story you have recently read. Make up a different ending for it. How will it now end? Happily? Unexpectedly? Mysteriously? Some other way? Think how your ending will affect the characters in the story.
- Plan your ideas in rough, first and then review them. Are you happy with the new ending? Does it make sense in relation to the rest of the story? Is there anything you want to change? When you are happy with it, write a best copy.

UNIT 17 Alphabet Poems and Acrostics

> **Think ahead**
>
> What do you notice about the first letter of each line in the first poem? the second poem?

An alphabet of horrible habits

A is for Albert who makes lots of noise
B is for Bertha who bullies the boys
C is for Cuthbert who teases the cat
D is for Dilys whose singing is flat
E is for Enid who's never on time
F is for Freddy who's covered in slime
G is for Gilbert who never says thanks
H is for Hannah who plans to rob banks
I is for Ivy who slams the front door
J is for Jacob whose jokes are a bore
K is for Kenneth who won't wash his face
L is for Lucy who cheats in a race
M is for Maurice who gobbles his food
N is for Nora who runs about nude

From *It's funny when you look at it* by Colin West

Rainbow

R ain and sun together make the rainbow grow
A rching in the cloudy sky, see the colours glow
I ndigo and violet, bands of red and blue
N ow it's bold and brilliant, then it fades from view
B ridge of coloured ribbons – magic to behold
O ver field and factory … over wood and wold
W here the rainbow comes to earth
          – there's the crock of gold

From *Poetry – Scholastic Collections* by David Whitehead

Thinking back

1 Why do you think the first poem is called an ALPHABET poem?
2 Why do you think the second poem is called an ACROSTIC poem?
3 Are the poems rhyming or non-rhyming poems?
4 Write the pairs of rhyming words in the alphabet poem.
5 Which poem is humorous and which poem is serious?

Thinking about it

1 Finish the second part of the alphabet poem. Here are some names you might have difficulty with: Olive, Quentin, Una, Victor, Xerxes, Youssef, Zoe. (Use copymaster 17 to help you plan it in rough first.)
2 Copy and finish this poem. (It does not have to rhyme.)
   G hastly noises
   H aunted houses
   O ld castles
   S
   T

Thinking it through

1 Write an alphabet poem, involving adjectives and verbs. Use the idea below. (Use a dictionary to help if you get stuck.)
   My cat is <u>a</u>ffectionate and is called <u>A</u>rchie. It loves <u>a</u>cting.
2 Choose one of these words and compose an acrostic poem. You may wish to make it rhyme, but it does not have to.
   a) your name   b) FIRE   c) HOLIDAYS   d) STORM

Stepping Stones to help you

- Firstly, brainstorm ideas and jot them down in rough.
- Experiment with them. Don't be afraid to change them.
- Choose your best ideas and make a best copy of your piece of work.

(Use copymaster C.)

UNIT 18   Conversation Poems

> **Think ahead**
>
> Many poems contain conversations. How do you know when the characters in this poem are speaking?

Cows

*Half the time they munched the grass, and all the time they lay
Down in the water-meadows, the lazy month of May,
A-chewing, A-mooing, to pass the hours away.*

"Nice weather," said the brown cow,
"Ah," said the white.
"Grass is very tasty,"
"Grass is all right."

*Half the time they munched the grass, and all the time they lay
Down in the water-meadows, the lazy month of May,
A-chewing, A-mooing, to pass the hours away.*

"Rain coming," said the brown cow,
"Ah," said the white.
"Flies is very tiresome,"
"Flies bite."

*Half the time they munched the grass, and all the time they lay
Down in the water-meadows, the lazy month of May,
A-chewing, A-mooing, to pass the hours away.*

"Time to go," said the brown cow,
"Ah," said the white.
"Nice chat." "Very pleasant."
"'Night." "'Night."

Cows by James Reeves

Thinking back

1 Who is the conversation in the poem between?
2 Where does the conversation take place?
3 Copy the chorus of the poem (the lines that are repeated three times).
4 Write down any rhyming words in the poem.
5 List some other things the cows might see and talk about.

Thinking about it

1 Make up four more lines for this animal poem. Notice which lines rhyme.
   The snake said, "I slide."
   The bird said, "I glide."
   The mouse said, "I creep."
   The deer said, "I leap."
2 Now make up four more lines for this animal poem. Notice which lines rhyme.
   The cat said, "I purr."
   The lion said "I roar."
   The owl said, "I hoot."
   The hedgehog said, "I snore."

Thinking it through

1 Make up your own verses to finish off this conversation poem.
   Ten tall trees, standing in a line,
      "Building planks," said Henry. Then there were nine.
   Nine tall trees, standing up straight,
      "Furniture," said Emily. Then there were eight.
2 See copymaster 18 for other ideas for writing conversation poems.

UNIT 19   Expressing a Point of View

> **Think ahead**
>
> *When you express a point of view, mention several positive things to support your opinion. Also mention some things other people think who do not agree with you, to give another viewpoint. What is Shireen expressing an opinion on, below?*

Charlotte is a new girl. Shireen wants to make her feel welcome, so she tells her what she thinks of the school.

Welcome to our school, Charlotte. I'm sure you'll like it because it's a lovely school. Most of the teachers are very nice and do interesting things. Each year the whole school goes on a school trip together. I stay for school dinners. I think they are as good as my mum's! If you like sport, you'll be glad to hear that our school has lots of after-school sports clubs. However, there are some children who like to moan! Although some say our playground is too small and the toilets are a bit smelly, I believe our school is the best in town. I'm sure you'll be very happy here.

Thinking back

1. What is Shireen expressing an opinion on?
2. Does Shireen begin with a positive or negative comment?
3. List some of the points Shireen makes in favour of the school.
4. List the things some people don't like.
5. Does Shireen finish with a positive or a negative comment?

Thinking about it

Imagine a new boy has just arrived at your school. What would you say about your school to him? Express a positive opinion about your school, like Shireen's. Before you begin, get your ideas together first. In rough, list some positive points about your school. Suggest some evidence to support your viewpoint. Also write a couple of negative things that people (who have a different opinion from yours) might say. Use copymaster 19 to help you set out your point of view.

Thinking it through

Choose one of these topics and write an argument in support of your point of view.
a) fast food is not good for you
b) everyone should bring a packed lunch to school
c) travelling by train is better than travelling by plane.

Stepping Stones to help you

- State your point of view at the beginning.
- Give several reasons to support your point of view.
- Mention some other points of view.
- Finish by re-stating and justifying your opinion

(Use copymaster O.)

UNIT 20 Writing a Letter

Think ahead

We can express our point of view in many ways. For example, we can do it face to face, in a debate, as a letter, in a report. In what form is the point of view below written?

Tom loves football but has got fed up with his local team. He has decided to write to the director of the club and state his point of view.

14 Stapleford Road
Lanchester
LU2 8RX

Dear Mr Hall

I have been a Lanchester Rovers supporter for several years, but I have become very unhappy with some developments lately.

Firstly, I do not feel you should change the club strip each year. It's very expensive for supporters to have to buy one every year.

Secondly, the cost of tickets has risen far too high. How can children afford to come to the matches any more?

I am also unhappy about the food you serve at the ground. It is often cold and greasy!

I know you are trying hard to create a family atmosphere at the club and to attract top class players, but unless you do a lot more for the spectators you will find many more people becoming unhappy and beginning to stay at home.

Yours sincerely

Tom Brown (aged 9)

➡ *Thinking back*

1. a) Who wrote the letter?
   b) Why do you think he put his age?
2. Who is the letter written to?
3. What is the purpose of the letter – is it a letter of complaint or support?
4. Write the reasons Tom gives for his unhappiness.
5. What does Tom say in support of the club?

➡ *Thinking about it*

Think of, and list in rough:
a) some other reasons why Tom might be unhappy with the football club (such as not enough seating for spectators, not enough cover for people in bad weather, cost of getting to the ground).
b) some other good things Tom might say (such as cut-price tickets for elderly, good facilities for the disabled).

Use some of your ideas and compose a different letter from Tom to Mr Hall. (Use copymaster 20 to help you plan your letter.)

➡ *Thinking it through*

Choose one of the following and compose a letter of complaint. Don't forget to say one or two positive things as well!
a) Imagine you were unhappy with several things about your local leisure centre. Write to Mrs I N Charge, the centre manager.
b) Imagine you received a board game for your birthday. (Make up your own name for the game.) You find there are three things wrong with it. Write to Mr G Damage, the company director.

Stepping Stones to help you

- State your point of view at the beginning.
- Give several reasons to support your point of view.
- Mention some other points of view.
- Finish by re-stating and justifying your opinion.

(Use copymaster K to help you.)

UNIT 21   Writing a Summary

> ### Think ahead
> *A summary is a short version of what someone has written or said. We only note the main ideas and miss out the details. Why do you think summaries are helpful?*

Towns are busy places where people meet. They might shop or work there. They might go to school or college there. People might go there for leisure or sport. Lots of people live in towns but some people just visit them.

People travel to towns in different ways. How they travel depends on how far they have to go and how much they can afford. Some towns have railways and bus links. Some towns are close to motorways. Some towns have canals. Some bigger towns and cities may have an airport.

Centuries ago people travelled along rough roads and tracks. Where these crossed they began to meet and exchange things. These meeting places became markets. Gradually people began to live and work near market places. These often grew into small towns.

Sometimes towns grew by rivers where there was a safe place to cross. Place names which contain 'bridge' and 'ford' in them, tell that they are by a river crossing. Cambridge and Oxford are examples.

Tara is writing a summary of the passage. She is writing down what the main idea of each paragraph is.

Summary
Many people live in towns because they are meeting places.
There are many different ways of travelling to towns.
Some towns…

Thinking back

1 Copy and complete this definition.
   A summary is a _____ version of what someone has written or said. We only note the _____ _____ and _____ _____ the details.
2 Explain why you think a summary is helpful.
3 Write what you think is the main idea of:
   a) the third paragraph   b) the fourth paragraph

Thinking about it

1 a) Copy this paragraph. Underline any important words or ideas.
     The fog caused lots of problems on the roads. There were long tailbacks of traffic on the roads into town. No aeroplanes were able to land or take off at the airport. Trains were delayed, causing many people to be late for work.
  b) Now say which of these tell you what the paragraph was mainly about: – fog   – traffic   – the effects of fog on travellers
2 Copy this paragraph. Underline any important words or ideas. Then write one sentence, giving the main idea of the paragraph.
     In the days gone by travelling was not easy. It was also very slow. Roads were very bad. There could be huge holes in them. They were often just mud tracks. In dry weather they could be very dusty. No-one was responsible for looking after them. If a tree fell across the road, no-one would bother to clear it!

Thinking it through

1 Practise your skills further with copymaster 21.
2 Here is a summary of a passage on health. The passage contained three paragraphs.
     The passage explained the need for physical exercise.
     It also stressed the importance of eating a healthy diet.
     Different aspects of keeping ourselves clean were discussed.
  a) In rough, write some notes on what details each paragraph might have contained.
  b) Based on your notes, make up the three short paragraphs which the summary describes.

UNIT 22 Composing an Advertisement

Think ahead
Many advertisements are designed to persuade you to buy something. How successful do you think this advertisement is?

The New taste sensation!

Chock Chip
The ice cream on a stick

- Use of adjectives
- Tempting picture of product
- Product appeals to all ages
- Famous pop star
- Catchy jingle
- Catchy slogan

"It's great!" "It's scrummy!" "It's smooth!" "It's tasty!" "It's cool!" "It's yummy!"

Chock Chip - a treat for the whole family

"I scream, you scream, we all scream for Spicers' ice creams!"

Spicers make good ices - just for you

➡️ *Thinking back*

1. a) What product is being advertised?
   b) How does the advert make this clear?
2. a) Who is the product aimed at – children, parents or older people?
   b) How does the advert make this clear?
3. List some of the adjectives used to describe the ice cream.
4. Why do you think a pop star is used to promote the product?
5. List a jingle or slogan used on the advert.

➡️ *Thinking about it*

Imagine you have just made a new type of crisp called 'Crunchy Crinkles'. Use copymaster 22 to plan an advert for your product. Try out your ideas in rough in pencil first. Don't be afraid to cross them out or change them. When you are happy with your ideas, make a best copy. Display it and ask for people's opinions about it. Ask for ideas on how it might be further improved.

➡️ *Thinking it through*

Compose a poster either:
a) for a school event (like a fete) or
b) to persuade people to keep your school litter-free.

Stepping Stones to help you

- Make it clear what you are advertising. Include its name and a picture.
- Include some facts or claims. Use interesting adjectives to make it sound exciting.
- Make it clear who the advert is aimed at.
- Use a snappy jingle or slogan.
- Don't put in too much detail.
- Make it bold, appealing and colourful.
- Think of ways of grabbing the reader's attention.

(Use copymaster P.)